THE CANADIAN
ROCKIES
BANFF, JASPER & BEYOND

John E. Marriott

Photography

All of the wildlife photographs in this book are of WILD, FREE-ROAMING ANIMALS.

LAKE O'HARA, *Yoho National Park* ▸
(*overleaf*) MOUNT LAWRENCE GRASSI *and Ha Ling Peak, Canmore, Alberta* ▸▸

Text and photographs copyright © 2009 by John E. Marriott

All rights reserved. No part of this book may be reproduced, stored in a retrieval system or transmitted in any form or by any means without the prior written consent of the publisher.

Library and Archives Canada Cataloguing in Publication

Marriott, John E., 1969–

    The Canadian Rockies : Banff, Jasper & beyond / written and photographed by John E. Marriott.

    ISBN 978-1-894768-03-0

1. Banff National Park (Alta.)--Pictorial works.
2. Jasper National Park (Alta.)--Pictorial works.
3. Rocky Mountains, Canadian (B.C. and Alta.)--Pictorial works.
4. Wilderness areas--Rocky Mountains, Canadian (B.C. and Alta.)--Pictorial works.
I. Title.

FC219.M37 2009   971.1'050222   C2009-902321-0

Published in Canada by
John E. Marriott, JEM PHOTOGRAPHY & PUBLISHING

info@wildernessprints.com
www.wildernessprints.com
1-877-774-3850 (*toll-free in North America*)
403-609-3850

Design, layout and colour work by
Richard Maruk, IVY DESIGN INC., CALGARY, ALBERTA

Editing by
Mike Potter,
LUMINOUS COMPOSITIONS, AIRDRIE, ALBERTA

Printing by
FRIESENS BOOK DIVISION, ALTONA, MANITOBA, CANADA

Acknowledgements:

I am grateful to Richard Maruk for the special commitment he made to this project and for his superb design work. Richard's continued dedication and interest in my book projects is vital to their success and for that he deserves singular recognition. Thank you also to Mike Potter for his timely and first-rate editing. Thanks to Janice Smith and Kim Weir with Parks Canada, and to Brian Patton, for their help researching the quotes found in this book. Finally, I would like to thank my friends and colleagues who provided feedback and support: Jennifer Cyr, Jason and Melissa Semenek, Kellie Woodford, Jordan Johnston, Richard Holgate, Nicky Lynch, Anne Frick, Dale and Colleen Dorion, Jakob Dulisse, Julius and Kristin Strauss, Thomas McIntyre, and Judy Hogg.

This book is printed on FSC-certified paper, an environmentally-friendly blend of recycled wood fibre and natural wood product from responsibly managed forests.

FSC
Mixed Sources
Product group from well-managed forests, controlled sources and recycled wood or fibre
Cert no. SW-COC-1271
www.fsc.org
© 1996 Forest Stewardship Council

Environmental Benefits Statement
Jem Photography saved the following resources by printing the pages of this book on chlorine free paper made with 10% post-consumer waste.

Trees 9 fully grown	Water 3,367 gallons	Energy 6 million BTUs
Solid Waste 558 pounds	Greenhouse Gases 1,031 pounds	

Calculations based on research by Environmental Defense and the Paper Task Force. Manufactured at Friesens Corporation

 **carbonzero**   *I am proud to announce that all emissions made during the printing, transportation, and distribution of this book, as well as all photographic travel in the last calendar year, have been offset with purchases from Carbonzero.*

in loving memory

CAROLINE HOLMES MARRIOTT 1938-2008.
THIS BOOK IS DEDICATED TO MY WONDERFUL MOM. *She loved the Canadian Rockies and spent many happy vacations here with my Dad enjoying the wildflowers at* SKOKI *and hiking at* LAKE O'HARA. *She gave me my first* SLR *camera,* HER BELOVED PENTAX ME SUPER, *and only occasionally joked afterwards that I should get a "real" job someday.*
THANK YOU, MOM, I MISS YOU MORE AND MORE EACH DAY.

"*There is told in the northwest the story of an old prospector of whom, returning after many years, it was asked what he had to show as the equivalent of so much lost time; and he answered only, 'I have seen the Rocky Mountains'.*"

J. Monroe Thorington
The Glittering Mountains

> *"That summer, my entire family piled into our old wood-paneled station wagon and drove the Icefields Parkway from Lake Louise to Jasper through what seemed like the most glorious wilderness in the world."*

———

THE PICTURE PROVES IT. The snapshot is fuzzy and grainy, but it still shows a very tiny me in the arms of my mother on the edge of the Columbia Icefield. It was my first visit to these hallowed mountains – August 1970 – but it would not be my last.

For as long as I can recall, the Canadian Rockies have played an integral role in my life. My first memories of the Rockies are from 1975, when I was just five years old. That summer, my entire family piled into our old wood-paneled station wagon and drove the Icefields Parkway from Lake Louise to Jasper through what seemed like the most glorious wilderness in the world.

I remember staring in awe at the towering mountain peaks that surrounded us, and I remember seeing seven black bears – including one that walked right in front of our car near Saskatchewan Crossing. I think from that moment onwards I was hooked on wild animals, on wild places, and most of all, on the wild Canadian Rocky Mountains.

Visiting the Rockies quickly became a family ritual. Each summer we would again load up the station wagon and head to one of our favourite national park campgrounds, camping along the Kicking Horse River in Yoho, at the Columbia Icefield in Jasper, in McLeod Meadows in Kootenay, or at my favourite, Johnston Canyon campground in Banff.

In high school, life seemed to get too busy for our family vacations to the mountains, and slowly, I forgot about my childhood playground, and laid aside my dreams to one day live in the Canadian Rockies.

I returned to the Rockies as an adult for the first time in May, 1991. It was meant to be a weekend holiday to reconnect with my childhood roots after a decade away from the mountains. Instead, my May long weekend turned into a month, which somehow became a year, which then grew into a decade. In fact, my May long weekend in the Rockies continues to this day – easily the longest *'holiday'* on record!

Over the course of this *'holiday,'* I have had some remarkable experiences in the Canadian Rockies. Banff is where I saw my first grizzly bear and my first mountain lion. It's also where I did my first solo backpacking trip, a six-day trek into a wild, remote corner of the park where the Devon Lakes sit like tiny jewels in the magnificent alpine environs of Clearwater Pass.

Jasper is where I saw my first mountain caribou and my first wild wolf. And it's where I first learned that solo backpacking is not all sunshine and roses; that being lost in a blizzard in August off-trail in the John-John Creek Valley in the Brazeau region is *not* fun.

Kootenay National Park is where I went looking for animals the day I traded in my VW van to buy my first big telephoto lens. I saw my first badger (there are badgers in the Rockies?!) in Waterton Lakes National Park. And I photographed my first lynx in Kananaskis Country just south of my home in Canmore.

There is so much to experience in the Canadian Rockies that you can easily spend a lifetime enjoying new trails or searching out wildlife you have never seen. I am still looking for my first wolverine, still eagerly anticipating my first trip along the North Boundary Trail in Jasper, and still looking forward to the first time I climb Mount Temple near Lake Louise.

For those of you who live in the Canadian Rockies or have visited them, I hope the images in this book help you relive memories of your own firsts, whether it be your first bear sighting or the first mountain you ever climbed. And I hope the photographs stir you to revisit your favourite haunts, or, better yet, seek out new ones.

If you've never been here, then I hope this book inspires you to visit – to experience for yourself the beauty of the Canadian Rocky Mountains – for the very magical, and memorable, first time.

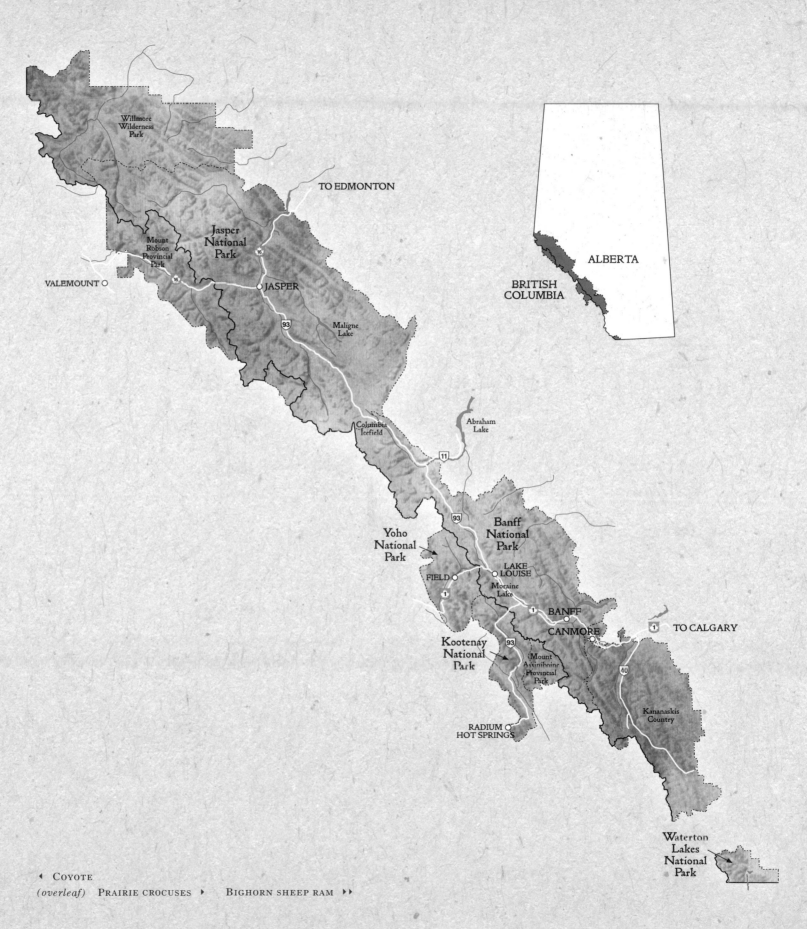

Willmore
Wilderness
Park

TO EDMONTON

Jasper
National
Park

Mount
Robson
Provincial
Park

16

VALEMOUNT ○

16

○ JASPER

93

Maligne
Lake

ALBERTA

BRITISH
COLUMBIA

09

Abraham
Lake

Columbia
Icefield

11

93

Banff
National
Park

Yoho
National
Park

LAKE
LOUISE ○

FIELD ○

Moraine
Lake

1

1

BANFF ○

CANMORE ○

TO CALGARY

Kootenay
National
Park

93

Mount
Assiniboine
Provincial
Park

40

RADIUM ○
HOT SPRINGS

Kananaskis
Country

Waterton
Lakes
National
Park

◄ Coyote
(overleaf) Prairie crocuses ► Bighorn sheep ram ►►

*"However, over an infinitesimally few those mountains had thrown
a glamour and a spell so persistent and so strong, that with the first
spring days, no matter where they be, warm breezes brought the call —
Come back, come back to the blue hills of the Rockies!"*

———

MARY SCHAFFER, early 20th century explorer of the Rockies
Old Indian Trails, 1911

SPRING IS A CAPTIVATING TIME OF YEAR IN THE
CANADIAN ROCKIES. With each day longer and warmer
than the one before, winter's icy grip fades, leaving in
its wake a shimmering, wet landscape brimming with
life. The bears are the first to emerge — big old males
trudging out of their dens in late March while the
snow is still deep, shaking off the cobwebs to wander
in search of food.

In April, the snows melt from the valley bottoms from
Waterton north to Jasper, and the first ground squirrels
appear, poking about in the brown grass for their first
morsels of the year. Prairie crocuses, a beautiful,
dainty purple flower, soon follow, a sure sign that
spring has officially arrived in the Rockies.

By May, the mountains are aglow with activity.
Beavers are actively working on their dams, baby
bears are frolicking about as their mothers feast on
the fresh green shoots bursting out along the roadsides, and new aspen buds are forming on the tips of
every branch.

June arrives, and so do elk calves, deer fawns, and
bighorn lambs. Babies seem to spring up everywhere.
And while they do, those final remnants of ice disap-
pear from our mountain lakes such as Peyto, Cavell,
and Louise, and we get to marvel once again at the
brilliant emeralds, blues, and greens.

13

14

Fresh spring snow, CLINE RIVER VALLEY *east of Banff National Park, Alberta* ▲
COW ELK *on the David Thompson Highway (# 11), Alberta* ▶

◂ *Fog along the slopes of* MOUNT WILSON, *Banff National Park*　　▴ GRAY WOLF

1883

Railway construction workers stumble across a cave containing hot springs near present-day Banff, leading to the creation of Banff National Park, Canada's first national park and the world's third. Today, Banff National Park spans more than 6,641 square kilometres (2,564 square miles) of mountains, lakes, rivers, and glaciers.

◂ *Dramatic storm cloud at sunrise*, Whiteman's Gap near Canmore, Alberta   ▴ Mount Fryatt *and the* Athabasca River, *Jasper National Park*

Glacier lily ▲   Grizzly bear cub ▶

◄ *Fresh* SPRING MELTWATER   ▲ WHITE-CROWNED SPARROW *in spring snowfall*

◂ *Cinnamon-coloured* BLACK BEAR CUB *clinging to a tree* ▴ COW ELK *scratching an itch on a lodgepole pine*

26

ATHABASCA FALLS *and* MOUNT KERKESLIN, *Jasper National Park* ◂   MOUNT RUNDLE *and* JOHNSON LAKE, *Banff National Park* ▸

28

Rainbow over the ICEFIELDS PARKWAY *during a rainstorm near Sunwapta Falls, Jasper National Park* ▲   THE THREE SISTERS *and the* BOW RIVER, *Canmore, Alberta* ▸

1754

ANTHONY HENDAY, a scout for the
fur-trading Hudson's Bay Company, becomes
the first European to ever set eyes on the
Canadian Rockies, when his party, led by
Cree guides, winters near the present-day city
of Red Deer, Alberta, in late 1754.

STELLER'S JAY ▲   WHIRLPOOL POINT *and the* NORTH SASKATCHEWAN RIVER, *Kootenay Plains, Alberta* ▶
(overleaf)   WILD LUPINE *near Valemount, British Columbia* ▶   COLUMBIAN GROUND SQUIRREL ▶▶

*"This is what I have seen in my dreams,
this is the country for me."*

———

JOHN GEORGE 'KOOTENAI' BROWN, early frontiersman and forest ranger
describing his first visit to the Waterton Lakes area, 1865

EACH SUMMER IN THE CANADIAN ROCKIES, the mountains come alive with an array of wildflower colours. Alpine meadows, old burns, avalanche slopes, riversides, and roadsides sport the brilliant reds, yellows, pinks, and purples of paintbrush, arnica, fireweed, and more.

While flowers are sprouting up everywhere, so is wildlife, as mule deer fawns roam the streets of Waterton townsite, and bighorn lambs frolic along the Icefields Parkway at Tangle Hill.

By mid-summer, every nook and cranny of the Rockies is open to the adventurous. Rock climbers dot one peak, mountain goats the next. Backpackers find themselves with a myriad of choices as high mountain passes become accessible. Even the tiniest, highest mountain lake becomes ice-free for a month or two.

In August, when the flowers begin to die off and berry season kicks into full gear, fortunate visitors can spot black or grizzly bears feasting on the sweet bounty in the valley bottoms. Meanwhile, bull moose brandish their newly-formed antlers in the high meadows, rubbing long strands of velvet off in preparation for the fall rut.

September arrives, bringing with it late summer snow-storms interspersed with long stretches of the crisp, cloud-free days of Indian summer. The landscape subtly fades from a rainbow of greens, blues, and yellows towards the browns of autumn.

Summer

Cotton grass below MOUNT ATHABASCA *and the* ATHABASCA GLACIER, *Jasper National Park* ▲   SUNSHINE MEADOWS, *Banff National Park* ▶

1984

THE CANADIAN ROCKY MOUNTAIN
PARKS WORLD HERITAGE SITE is designated
by the United Nations. It includes Banff,
Jasper, Yoho, and Kootenay national parks,
as well as Mount Robson, Mount Assiniboine,
and Hamber provincial parks.

▸ BIGHORN SHEEP HERD *in Piper Pass, Kananaskis Country*   ▸ SPIRIT ISLAND *and* MALIGNE LAKE, *Jasper National Park*

◄ Mule deer fawn, *Waterton townsite, Waterton Lakes National Park*   ▲ Mount Lorette *and the* Kananaskis River, *Kananaskis Country*

325

The Columbia Icefield is the Rockies' largest icefield, covering more than 325 square kilometres (125 square miles), with ice as thick as 365 metres (1,197 feet). It is the hydrographic apex of North America; snow melting from a summit called the Snow Dome drains to three different oceans: the Atlantic, the Pacific, and the Arctic.

◄ Dome Glacier, *Jasper National Park*   ▲ Moraine Lake, *Banff National Park*

42

BLACK BEAR *eating dandelions* ▴

▲ *Wildflowers* in Molar Pass, *Banff National Park*

WHITE-TAILED PTARMIGAN *molting into summer plumage* ▲   *West Fork of the* LITTLE ELBOW RIVER VALLEY, *Kananaskis Country* ▶

CASTLE MOUNTAIN *and the* BOW RIVER, *Banff National Park* ◄   MOUNTAIN GOAT NANNY *and* KID ►

WESTERN ANEMONE SEEDHEADS ▲   CAVELL POND *and* ANGEL GLACIER, *Jasper National Park* ▸

1.5

SINCE IT WAS DISCOVERED JUST OVER ONE
HUNDRED YEARS AGO, the Athabasca Glacier
has lost more than half its volume and receded
more than 1.5 kilometres (0.93 miles) as a
result of global warming. Much of the terrain
that used to be covered by the glacier has
now been colonized by wildflowers and
other flora.

◄ NORTHERN SWEETVETCH *and* MOUNT ATHABASCA, *Jasper National Park*   ▲ FIREWEED *and* BOW LAKE, *Banff National Park*

Waterfall on Opabin Plateau, *Schaffer Ridge, Yoho National Park* ▲   Pyramid Lake *and* Pyramid Mountain, *Jasper National Park* ▶

54

Emerald Lake, *Yoho National Park* ▲   Lake O'Hara, Cathedral Mountain, *and* Wiwaxy Peaks, *Yoho National Park* ▶

57

◂ SPILLWAY LAKE, *Kananaskis Country*   ▴ MARSH MARIGOLD *and the headwaters of* MOSQUITO CREEK, *Banff National Park*

58

THE RAMPARTS *and* AMETHYST LAKES, *Tonquin Valley, Jasper National Park* ▲ MOUNT ASSINIBOINE, *Mount Assiniboine Provincial Park* ▶
(overleaf) BEARBERRY LEAVES *in fall colours* ▶ MUSKRAT *eating a reed* ▶▶

*"The mountains now increase to a stupendous size;
the summits of many obscured from our sight by clouds and
of others covered by eternal snows."*

———

George Simpson, explorer, describing his trip on the Athabasca Trail in October, 1824
Fur Trade and Empire – George Simpson's Journal, 1931

The first weeks of autumn are the most brilliant. As September draws to a close, the aspen forests that clothe the foothills and line the great valleys of the Athabasca and Bow Rivers turn shimmering shades of yellow and orange to welcome the start of the fall season.

The subalpine larch, which carve out a tenuous existence at treeline, also undergo an eye-catching transformation. Their pale green needles turn radiant gold, lighting up regions such as Lake O'Hara in Yoho National Park and Highwood Pass in Kananaskis Country.

Willows in the valley bottoms do their best to keep up, showcasing varied hues of orange and red. Even the meadow grasses transform into beautiful shades of gold and brown, providing picturesque arenas for the bugling bull elk as they battle for supremacy.

With the shorter days come cooler temperatures and morning frosts. By mid-October, the colours are gone, as are most of the human visitors. Wolf packs travel the empty roadways, and bull moose begin their rut in earnest.

Snow comes and goes, lingering longer each time, while ice begins to form on the ponds and high elevation lakes. By the time November arrives, the Canadian Rockies lie cold and barren, in a state of dormancy, in preparation for the long winter ahead.

Fall

Marble Canyon, *Kootenay National Park* ◄   Prince of Wales Hotel, *Waterton Lakes National Park* ►

PIKA ▲

▲ FALL COLOURS

◄ CROSS RIVER FALLS *near Radium, British Columbia*   ▲ SHRUBBY CINQUEFOIL, LAKE LOUISE, *and* FAIRVIEW MOUNTAIN, *Banff National Park*

Bull moose *in autumn snowfall* ▲   Mount Temple, *Banff National Park* ▸

Young GRAY WOLF ▲   SUBALPINE LARCHES *on Opabin Plateau, Mount Huber, Yoho National Park* ▶

3954

MOUNT ROBSON is the tallest peak in the Canadian Rockies at 3,954 metres (12,969 feet). In their 1865 account, *The Northwest Passage by Land,* early adventurers Viscount Milton and W.B. Cheadle wrote that Robson was "a giant among giants, and immeasurably supreme."

◄ MOUNT ROBSON *and the* ROBSON VALLEY, *Mount Robson Provincial Park* ▲ TREMBLING ASPEN

74

MOOSE MEADOWS, *Banff National Park* ▲   MOUNT ASSINIBOINE, *Mount Assiniboine Provincial Park* ▶

1907

JASPER NATIONAL PARK is established by the
Dominion of Canada. Jasper is the largest
national park in the Canadian Rockies at
10,878 square kilometres (4,200 square miles)
and includes Alberta's tallest mountain,
Mount Columbia, at 3,747 metres (12,293 feet).

◄ Tonquin Valley, *Jasper National Park* ▲ Larch Valley *and* Mount Temple, *Banff National Park*

LAKE LOUISE, *Banff National Park* ▲ PORCUPINE

Alpenglow on the east face of MOUNT RUNDLE *from Canmore, Alberta* ▲

▲ *Sunrise over the* TRANS-CANADA HIGHWAY (#1) *from Castle Junction, Banff National Park*
(overleaf) HOAR FROST *on a willow branch* ▸ GREAT GRAY OWL ▸▸

> *"Their pointed & snowy summits rose high into the heavens*
> *like the lofty spires of some vast & magnificent marble temple...*
> *The sight seemed too grand & too glorious for reality."*

> REVEREND ROBERT T. RUNDLE, describing the Rockies near Banff in 1841
> *The Rundle Journals,* 1840-1848

Winter in the Canadian Rockies is long, cold, and bitter, yet it's also a wonderful season. Few things can compare in beauty to a crisp, blue sky day in December, myriad sparkling snow particles sprinkled liberally in each meadow and on every tree – the entire landscape a winter wonderland.

Icicles hang like crystal daggers, and mist rises from open water, coating the riverside willows in hoar frost. Bull elk gather in the meadows and forage, digging deep into the snow to salvage what they can, each breath visible against the morning sun.

The heart of winter arrives in January, when snow falls regularly in big, luscious flakes, coating the mountains in soft blankets of white. Skates, skis, and snowshoes become a mode of exercise and adventure in the cool temperatures.

The snow tells many stories in winter. One can see numerous tales in the tracks, such as where a wolf pack crossed the road the night before, where a lynx chased down a snowshoe hare, or where a pine marten ventured up to a backcountry hut to nestle against a warm outer wall.

By March, the first inklings of spring arrive. Temperatures rise above freezing and the snow begins to melt. But then another storm arrives, bringing with it new snow and proving that winter is not quite over.

Winter

TANGLE FALLS, *Jasper National Park* ▲   GRAY WOLF ▶

◀ MALIGNE RIVER, *Jasper National Park* ▲ MULE DEER DOE

Bow River *and the* Sawback Range, *Banff National Park* ◂   Castle Mountain *and the* Bow River, *Banff National Park* ▸

1858

Sir James Hector, geologist for the
Palliser Expedition, was still 19 kilometres
from the base of Castle Mountain when he
named it in 1858. Hector described the
distinct peak, 2,766 metres (9,076 feet) tall, as
a "remarkable mountain… which looks
exactly like a giant castle."

Winter mist on the BOW RIVER, *Banff National Park* ▲

▲ Second Vermilion Lake *and* Mount Rundle, *Banff National Park*

BULL ELK *in a snowstorm* ▲   OPAL RANGE, *Kananaskis Country* ▶

Haffner Creek Falls, *Kootenay National Park* ▲   *Moonset over* Mount Lougheed, *near Canmore, Alberta* ▸
(overleaf) Subalpine larches *and* Schaffer Ridge, *Yoho National Park* ▸

*"…Looking west, I beheld the great range in unclouded glory…
a mighty barrier rising midst an immense land, standing sentinel over
the plains and prairies… Here, at last, lay the Rocky Mountains."*

W.F. BUTLER, soldier and adventurer
The Great Lone Land, 1872

To read some of the stories behind JOHN'S PHOTOGRAPHS,
visit his website at www.wildernessprints.com